THE GRILL COOKBOOK

Easy, delicious and flavorful
Mexican Grill Recipes
to Enjoy with Your Family and Friends

Joe Sullivan

The following Book is reproduced below with the goal of providing information that is as accurate and reliable as possible. Regardless, purchasing this Book can be seen as consent to the fact that both the publisher and the author of this book are in no way experts on the topics discussed within and that any recommendations or suggestions that are made herein are for entertainment purposes only. Professionals should be consulted as needed prior to undertaking any of the action endorsed herein.

This declaration is deemed fair and valid by both the American Bar Association and the Committee of Publishers Association and is legally binding throughout the United States.

Furthermore, the transmission, duplication, or reproduction of any of the following work including specific information will be considered an illegal act irrespective of if it is done electronically or in print. This extends to creating a secondary or tertiary copy of the work or a recorded copy and is only allowed with the express written consent from the Publisher. All additional right reserved.

The information in the following pages is broadly considered a truthful and accurate account of facts and as such, any inattention, use, or misuse of the information in question by the reader will render any resulting actions solely under their purview. There are no scenarios in which the publisher or the original author of this work can be in any fashion deemed

Table of Contents

Introduction

Grilling is one of the most original forms of cooking. If the kitchen is moved outside when the outside temperature is pleasant, the dishes prepared in this way taste even better. In addition, there is a very special feeling of being together and preparing food together. Grilling was never really out of fashion, but has experienced a real boom in recent years, which is related to various cookery programs on TV and the large grill manufacturers who keep bringing new devices and products onto the market and thus for an ever-expanding spectrum Provide opportunities and methods.

Grilling

In the original sense, the term "grilling" refers to roasting over an open fire. When grilling, the grilled food is cooked by radiant heat and roasted on the surface. In addition to the roasted substances, this process also creates the aroma typical of grilling.

Which Grill Is The Right One? - Presentation Of The Different Types Of Barbecues

Opinions are divided on this question. There are 100%

supporters of charcoal and equally enthusiastic supporters of modern gas grills. So that you can get a more detailed picture of the various grills and their special technology, we would like to show you to the most important grills:

- charcoal grill

The charcoal grill or charcoal grill is the epitome of the grill for many. Glowing fans of this type of grill are convinced that grilling with charcoal creates a distinctive taste. However, numerous studies show that with the classic preparation process, there is no great difference in taste between the food on the charcoal grill and that on the gas grill. It is, however, the case that when grilling on charcoal, dripping fat or other liquids can fall on the embers, causing additional smoke to settle on the grilled food. This creates a very special taste, but it is not good for your health.

Make sure that no fat drips into the embers when using a charcoal grill.

To refine the barbecue enjoyment when using a charcoal grill, you can add special smoking chips or watered wood shavings (e.g. walnut or fruit woods such as cherry) to the embers. The smoke that you generate in this way is very aromatic, contributes to a special taste and is harmless to health.

A special highlight of the charcoal grill is the smell that arises when grilling with charcoal and does not appear when grilling with gas.

There are numerous versions of charcoal grills in stores: The range on offer ranges from very small disposable grills to inexpensive models in many formats and luxury designs in various sizes.

When purchasing a charcoal grill, it is advisable to make sure that the grill has a lid. A lid is particularly necessary for indirect grilling, as otherwise, the heat cannot be retained.

Well-equipped charcoal grills allow you to use the grill grate at different heights to regulate the heat. Variably adjustable ventilation slots are also very useful in this context. If you let more air into the embers, this means more heat, while restricting the air supply reduces the temperature somewhat. Regardless of the features of the charcoal grill, its temperature can also be controlled via the amount of charcoal used.

- The kettle grill - a special design

Classic kettle grills are designed as charcoal grills. Since this design is now enjoying great popularity, kettle grills are also offered with the gas operation.

The kettle grill was originally invented to prevent the fat from the grill from dripping into the embers and causing them to burn. However, other advantages of this design were soon discovered, such as excellent stability.

Due to its characteristic shape, the kettle grill is ideal for the preparation of many different grilled goods. For example, it is no problem to cook a thick T-bone steak or a whole chicken on this grill.

A kettle grill is usually made up of two hemispheres: The lower part (often with a mobile stand) is used to hold the coals (with a charcoal grill), whereby these are placed on their own grate, which provides additional ventilation from below, whereby the Development of an even heat is possible. The actual grill grate is in a slightly raised position above the charcoal grate. Ball grills are often used in this context for indirect grilling. Accordingly, it is not grilled directly over the coals. First and foremost, the warm air and smoke are used for cooking the food to be grilled. The top part of the kettle grill is the lid. This can also be provided with additional practical equipment such as a thermometer or adjustable ventilation openings.

Ball grills can, of course, not only be used for the indirect grilling process but also for grilling directly over the embers.

- Gas grill - grilling with gas

Gas grills generate hot air, which is then used for grilling. One of the advantages of gas grills is that they are very easy to light and very easy to regulate. In addition, the desired temperature can be reached fairly quickly with the gas grill, which saves time compared to the charcoal grill.

Gas bottles for operating such grills are available in various sizes in stores and are easy to get, which is why frequent grill use is not a problem at all. For unadulterated barbecue enjoyment and for the greatest possible flexibility and spontaneity, it is advisable to always have a filled replacement bottle in the house.

Gas grills are built in different ways: There are grills that use lava stones or ceramic briquettes. These are quickly heated up by the burning gas and then transfer to the heat to the food to be grilled. In addition, the lava stones or ceramic briquettes also catch the dripping fat. In other model variants of this grill type, the gas flames heat rods made of special steel or cast iron, which are located under the actual grill grate, which absorbs and release the heat.

Gas barbecues are usually equipped with two or, ideally, even more burners, which allow good control over where in the grill a particularly large amount of direct heat should be available.

Most grills that run on gas are usually very generous in size so that four to six people can be supplied with delicious grill specialities at the same time without any problems. In addition, there are of course also models with a particularly large grill area, which is ideal for parties and other events, as well as very space-saving variants that are easy to transport and, for example, provide good service on the campsite.

Almost all gas grills are equipped with lids. When closed, they keep the heat very well and also offer a wide range of uses.

- Table Grill / Electric Grill

The table grill or electric grill can also be used without any problems within the apartment, regardless of the weather and season. You only need a socket for its operation. Another advantage of the table grill / electric grill is that no smoke is generated when it is used so that the neighbours are not disturbed when used outside on the balcony.

Table grills / electric grills are usually only suitable for indirect grilling to a limited extent so that traditional direct grilling is used here.

In terms of size, most table grills / electric grills are rather short, so that larger groups of people can only be supplied with a single device with great difficulty. For this reason, it is our recommendation for rainy days and a small number of people.

- Dutch oven

The Dutch Oven is not an everyday grill device, which is wonderful as a second device or additional grill. It is a cast-iron pot with a lid. Usually, the pot is placed on a suitable stand, which stands directly in glowing coals. In addition, glowing coals are placed on the lid of the Dutch Oven. In this way, heat is evenly transferred to the food placed in the pot so that it is prepared gently, and all of the aromatic substances are retained.

The Dutch Oven gets very hot when it is used, which is why it must be handled with care. In this context, the trade offers Dutch Oven grill sets which, in addition to one or more pots in different sizes, also include useful accessories such as a lid lifter.

Due to its nature and use, the Dutch Oven is ideal for indirect grilling. How many people can be "fed up" with it depends, among other things, on its size and the grilled food used.

What Grill Methods Are There?

If you deal with the topic of grilling, you will almost automatically be confronted with the terms direct grilling and indirect grilling. There are differences between the two grill methods; explain the advantages and disadvantages and give you a lot of additional information.

- Direct grilling

The direct grilling method is the classic method of grilling. Here the grilled food is cooked in a short time at high temperatures from approx. 250 ° C. Depending on the kind technology used, the distance between the food to be grilled and the heat source is adjusted as required. When grilling directly, the typical brown crust is created on the food.

Since the direct grilling process "works" at high temperatures, the cooking times are short.

Basically, all grilled food with a cooking time of <30 minutes is suitable for direct grilling. This includes, for example, steaks in any shape, chops, sausages, skewers and various vegetables.

You should rather refrain from deglazing with beer, as this process creates additional smoke or soot, which is deposited on the grilled food, which is said to be hazardous to health.

Depending on the nature of the grillage, the heat generated by the direct grilling process creates a deliberate "drawing" on the meat surface. This is also known as branding. The best results can be achieved in this context with cast iron grills, as these distribute the heat extremely evenly.

- Indirect grilling

For example, indirect grilling is often used when using a kettle grill. With this method, the food is not positioned directly over the charcoal. Instead, the heat acts equally on meat, vegetables, etc., from all sides.

For indirect grilling, a bowl filled with water is placed under the food to be grilled. It serves to catch the dripping fat. In this way, the humidity in the closed grill is significantly higher, which means that meat, for example, is tender and juicy. If you want to influence the taste of indirect grilling, you can also fill the fat drip tray with wine or beer instead of water.

Gas grills are also suitable for indirect grilling: the gas grill is preheated before the food is placed on the grill. If you put meat, fish and Co. on the grill, you switch off the burners, which are located directly below. The lid of the gas grill is then kept closed for indirect grilling, as when using a kettle grill or similar charcoal grill model.

What Care Does The Grill Need?

If you do not need the grill, you should always store it in a dry place, regardless of its type. It does not matter whether you place a coal or gas grill in a garden shed, tool shed, in the basement or in a storage room. If there is no such space available, you should at least get a suitable protective cover or cover that protects the grill from the elements.

When grilling, juice and fat come out of the grilled food, ash and residues are formed, and leftovers stick to the grillage. Cleaning the grill is therefore essential for long-term

barbecuing pleasure. In the Wohnen.de magazine, we explain what you should look out for when using charcoal barbecues, gas barbecues and when cleaning the grill grate:

- Clean and maintain the charcoal grill

After using a charcoal grill, all residues such as the cold ash and the cooled charcoal must be disposed of. Make sure that there really is nothing left to glow. To be on the safe side, you can wait until the next day. Then, sweep the charcoal area of the grill with an old broom or hand brush.

- Clean and care for the gas grill

When grilling on the gas grill, the gas supply must, of course, be turned off. After the gas grill has cooled down, empty the drip trays for the fat and wash them out with hot water and a splash of detergent. Use a damp cloth to clean the grill bars. Remove any food particles that have fallen down. Also, check to see if the torch or nozzles are clogged. If there is a blockage, thorough cleaning is also advisable here. After cleaning the gas grill with a damp cloth, you should reheat it briefly afterwards so that any moisture that may have remained evaporates and rust cannot form.

If your gas grill has lava stones, you can boil them in vinegar water once or twice a year to remove fat and other residues.

- Clean and care for the grill grate

The grill grate is the most stressed when grilling. Usually, after grilling, some food and fat residues adhere to the grate and have to be removed. If you want to clean the grate when it is cold, this is not really an easy job. Ideally, you should dedicate yourself to cleaning the grate immediately after grilling. Take the grate off the fire while it is still warm. Use the grill tongs to grab a cloth soaked in oil and rub it firmly over the grillage. With the oil, you not only lay the foundation for optimal grilling results the next time you use it but also protect it from corrosion.

Mexican grilled pork

15 mins

Ingredients for 4 people

600 g About grilled pork

2Lime

2 garlic cloves

2 tbsp. tablespoon Oil

2 or 3Tabasco drops

1 tsp. teaspoon Tomato paste

1 tsp. 1 teaspoon Fennel seeds

1 tsp. Coffee Sugar

Salt

Preparation

Cut each grilled pork into two pieces.

Prepare the marinade: in a large dish, put the previously crushed garlic cloves, fennel seeds, powdered sugar, lime juice, oil, tomato paste and Tabasco. Salt and stir.

Dip the grilled pork in this preparation, coating them well with the mixture and let them marinate for 1 hour, turning them several times so that they are well impregnated.

Drain the grills carefully and grill them for about 15 minutes, turning them halfway through cooking.

Serve very hot with lamb's lettuce and small corn cakes.

Tips and advice for Grilled Mexican pork

Limes give more juice if you cut them lengthwise rather than crosswise. In this case, squeeze them with a fork instead of using the juicer.

For a more distinctive recipe, you can replace the Tabasco with a small dry crushed pepper. In this case, wash your hands after handling the peppers as their contact can cause unpleasant burning sensations.

Wild fennel is found in the countryside. If you see any, stock up on it. You can use it fresh in meat or vegetable recipes and dry with fish.

To make the garlic more digestible , cut the cloves in half lengthwise and remove the green sprout with a knife.

Mexican marinated barbecue skewers

25min

Ingredients 4 people

4 pork chops

1 onion

0.5 lemon

3 tbsp. to s. olive oil

2 tbsp. to s. fresh coriander

1 C. to s. paprika

2 g of chili puree

Parsley

Salt or fine salt

Pepper

Equipment

Barbecue

Bowl

Preparation

Preparation: 10 minutes

Cooking: 15min

Expectation: 2h

Cut the pork into pieces in a salad bowl add the lemon juice, olive oil, onion, salt and pepper, paprika, chili puree 2 tbsp cilantro and parsley.

Chill for 2 hours and cook on the barbecue.

Mexican BBQ Chicken Recipe

Ingredients: 4 pers.

For the marinade:

-zest and juice of 2 large limes

-3 c. oil soup

-1 pinch of dried chilli

-2 tsp. finely chopped fresh cilantro

-2 cloves of garlic, finely chopped

-2 tsp. teaspoon paprika

-1 C. toasted cumin seeds

-salt

pepper

For the chicken:

-1 chicken cut into 4 portions

-1 can of black beans, drained

-2 tomatoes, diced

-2 stalks of celery, thinly sliced

-1 small red onion, minced

-1 large red pepper, diced

-1 clove of garlic, minced

-3 c. chopped fresh cilantro

-3 c. oil soup

-salt

-pepper

Preparation

1.Add all marinade ingredients inside a bowl.Incorporate the chicken and soak all the pieces.Let macerate for 2 hours in the refrigerator.Brais the barbecue at 2 intensities. Lightly lubricate the grates. Wring out the meat. Grill the chicken for 12 min on the high heat side of the barbecue. Arrange them on the side at low intensity. Close the lid and continue cooking for 12 minutes without forgetting to turn the meat. Heat the oil in a saucepan. Cook the celery, onion, bell pepper and garlic for 5 min. Add the cilantro, beans and diced tomatoes. Season and simmer the preparation for 5 minutes over low heat. Place your chicken on serving platter and cover it with the vegetable mixture.

Mexican marinade for chicken

Ingredients

3 tablespoons minced garlic cloves

2 teaspoons of oregano

1 tablespoon of paprika

2 teaspoons of cumin

1/4 cup (65 mL) orange juice

1/4 cup (65 mL) lime juice

1/2 teaspoon garlic powder

1/2 teaspoon cayenne pepper

1/4 cup (65 mL) olive oil

1/2 teaspoon of pepper

1 teaspoon of salt

Meat: 3 lbs of chicken

Preparation

Mix all the marinade ingredients well. Cover the meat with the marinade. Marinate for like 30 minutes, but ideally overnight. Bake at 400 ° F (200 ° C) for 25 minutes.

Grilled barbecue chicken, tarragon flavor, corn withlemon cream

Chicken with tarragon, barbecued corn, cream and lemon sauce

for 4 people

Preparation time: 20 min

Cooking time: 15/20 min

Total time: 40 min

Ingredients

4 boneless chicken breast pieces

3 ears of fresh corn (or tin can)

10 cl of fresh cream

juice of 1/2 lemon

milk

100g chopped fresh tarragon (or basil, depending on taste)

2 tbsp olive oil

1 tsp of smoked paprika

salt

Preparation

Inside a small bowl, combine the olive oil, tarragon, salt and paprika. Brush the corn and chicken with the oil mixture. Place directly on the grill or plancha (preheated material) for about 12 to 15 minutes. Remove, then peel the corn kernels using a sharp knife, then mix them with the cream topped with lemon and a little milk, until you get a creamy texture. Season with salt and pepper. Serve the grilled chicken pieces with the corn, sprinkle with chopped tarragon.

Beef nachos recipe

for 2 people:

250 g minced meat

1 tsp of ground cumin

2 tablespoons chopped onion

1 large garlic clove, crushed

150 ml tomato sauce

grated cheese (mozzarella or cheddar)

chili pepper, chopped to taste

pitted black olives, sliced into slices

salt and pepper

tortilla chips

Preparation

Brown the meat dry, add the onion and garlic, while stirring. When the onion is well translucent, add the tomato sauce and seasoning, then cook for a few minutes.

Arrange tortilla chips on a plate, pour in the meat, sprinkle with cheese, then melt for a few seconds in the microwave (or grill).

Mexican vegetable plancharecipe

For 4 people

Ingredients

1 pre-cooked corn on the cob

1 orange pepper - 1 zucchini

2 tomatoes + 4 candied tomatoes

a mixture of mushrooms (frozen this winter)

1 bowl of frozen peas

1 bowl of carrots (frozen this winter)

2 fresh green onions - 1 onion and 2 shallots

2 tablespoons of Mexican spices (coriander, cumin, oregano, parsley, paprika, hot pepper)

4 tortillas - olive oil + spray - salt

griddle to Simogas® stove or gas

Vegetable plancha

Preparation

Cut the pepper into strips, the zucchini into slightly thick slices and the tomatoes into 4 then 2 to obtain cubes.

Peel the onion and shallots and cut them into strips for the onion and cubes for the shallots.

Cut the candied tomatoes in 2, remove the carrots, peas and mushrooms from the freezer .

Prepare the Mexican marinade by mixing olive oil, Mexican spice blend and a little salt, then mix in the vegetables as they are cooked in order of cooking.

Cooking the vegetable plancha

Light the gas plancha on high heat for 5 minutes.

Apply a spray of olive oil and cook the carrots and peppers first.

As soon as they take color, add the onion, shallots and frozen mushrooms.

Stir often with the large spatulas to prevent the vegetables from sticking.

Reduce the gas to medium and now add the zucchini and candied tomatoes.

Stir several times then add the cubes of fresh tomatoes, peas and the ear of corn on the side.

Finish with the fresh green onions cut into 4 lengthwise.

Place the vegetable plancha in an oven dish and place it on the cooler side of the plancha just to keep them warm.

Finish cooking the corn on the cob on all sides so that it caramelizes.

Remove the corn on the cob and scrape the plancha to clean it from leftover vegetables.

Place the tortillas on low to heat them up if you want to make fajitas stuffed with Mexican vegetables.

Otherwise let them grill lightly and, while lukewarm, they will harden and serve as tortilla chips to eat with the vegetables.

Vegetable plancha recipe for 2 people

Ingredients

Organic zucchini : 2

Organic bell pepper : 1

Organic cherry tomatoes : 3

Candied tomatoes : 4

Fresh organic onion : 1

Organic eggs : 4

Feta : 20 grams

Olive oil and Oregano Terre2Crète®

Salt - Paprika

Preparation

Light the plancha and heat it for 5 minutes.

Wash the vegetables and dry them.

Cut the courgettes into slightly thick slices.

Make strips of peppers and fresh onion.

Cut the candied tomatoes and the cherry tomatoes in half.

Combine the vegetables on a plate with the olive oil, oregano and salt.

Place them on the hot plancha and using 2 large spatulas turn them regularly.

Break the eggs into a bowl and when the vegetables are done, gently pour the eggs over them.

Reduce the gas on the plancha and let the eggs cook gently.

Sprinkle the eggs with paprika before delicately removing them by passing the spatulas underneath.

Crumble the feta over the vegetables and the paprika eggs and go to the table!

Mozzarella salad, grilled vegetables a la plancha andbasil pesto

For 1 mozzarella salad

Preparation time: 10 minutes - Cooking time: 15 minutes

Ingredients

Mozzarella di bufala: 1 scoop

Organic eggplant : 1

Organic zucchini : 1

Organic green pepper : 1

Organic red pepper : 1

Organic basil : 10 leaves

Sprocket : 1 small handle

Olive oil : 2 tablespoons and coarse salt

Utensils:

mandolin, mortar and gas plancha

Cooking grilled vegetables in sliced eggplant, zucchini and basil pesto

Preparation

Light the plancha, grill the peppers on all sides, then place them in a plastic bag to create steam that will help remove the skin.

Cut the eggplant and zucchini into slices with the mandolin and cook them on the plancha with a drizzle of olive oil.

Pound the basil leaves, pine nuts, a little coarse salt and olive oil to make the pesto and keep in the fridge.

Place the mozzarella in cling film and steam it until the core becomes soft (2-3 minutes).

Warm mozzarella salad with grilled vegetables a la plancha and basil pesto

Dressing the mozzarella salad

Place the slices of zucchini, eggplant and strips of peppers in a nice white plate then place the warm bufala mozzarella in the center of the grilled vegetables.

Pour basil pesto on the grilled vegetables and on the mozzarella di bufala then sprinkle with some fresh basil leaves and pass to the table and for those who like, you can add shavings this Parmesan.

This warm mozzarella salad was a real treat in the restaurant and I am delighted to have been able to find all these flavors at home, it can be served as a starter or as a main cours

BBQ ranch eggs with blackbeans (huevos rancheros)

25 min

Cooking 25 min

Portions 4

Ingredients

420 g (3 cups) cherry tomatoes

1 serrano or jalapeño pepper, seeded and coarsely chopped

1 onion, chopped

1 yellow bell pepper, seeded and diced

2 garlic cloves, chopped

45 ml (3 tbsp.) Olive oil

5 ml (1 teaspoon) dried oregano

1/2 teaspoon (2.5 ml) ground cumin

15 ml (1 tbsp.) Red wine vinegar

1 can 19 oz (540 ml) black beans, rinsed and drained

4 eggs

80 g (2/3 cup) crumbled feta cheese

Coriander leaves, to taste

1 ripe avocado, diced (optional)

Preparation

Place a cast iron skillet about 25 cm (10 inches) in diameter and 5 cm (2 inches) high on the barbecue grill. Preheat on medium power.

Place the tomatoes and chili in the hot pan. Close barbecue lid and cook dry until tomatoes burst and release some juice, about 8 minutes, stirring twice. Reserve in a bowl.

In the same pan, soften the onion, pepper and garlic in the oil for 4 minutes, stirring with a wooden spoon. Add oregano and cumin. Continue cooking for 1 minute while stirring. Add the vinegar, black beans and two-thirds of the tomatoes. Salt and pepper.

Using a spoon, form 4 cavities in the mixture then break the eggs. Close the barbecue lid and cook for 6 minutes or until the egg whites are cooked through and the yolks are still runny. Remove the pan from the barbecue.

Season the eggs with salt and pepper. Top with remaining tomatoes, feta, cilantro and avocado. Serve with toasted corn tortillas, if desired.

Chicken stuffed tortillas(taquitos)

25 MIN

Cooking 15 min

Portions 4

Ingredients

Guacamole

1 large ripe avocado, peeled and pitted

1 lime, for juice

1 green onion, chopped

1/2 jalapeño pepper, seeded and chopped

Taquitos

340 g (2 cups) cooked chicken, coarsely chopped

100 g (1 cup) grated tex-mex cheese

2 green onions, thinly sliced

10 small soft wheat tortillas, 6 inches (15 cm) in diameter

30 ml (2 tbsp.) Canola oil

Side dishes (optional)

Iceberg lettuce, minced

Homemade or store-bought salsa

Sour cream

Preparation

Guacamole

In a bowl, get a fork, mash the avocado. Add lime juice, green onion and chili pepper. Add salt, pepper and mix well. Reserve.

Taquitos

In another bowl, place the chicken, cheese and green onions. Salt and pepper. With your hands or with a wooden spoon, mix vigorously until the preparation is a little pasty, even sticky.

On a work surface, place a few tortillas at a time. Spread about 45 ml (3 tbsp.) Of the chicken mixture inside the center of the bottom of each tortilla. Roll while pressing. To keep them rolled, prick each tortilla with a toothpick or thread a long skewer through 5 tortillas side by side. If the preparation escapes from the ends, simply push it back by pressing it towards the inside of the tortillas.

In a large non-stick skillet with medium heat, heat the oil. Place half the tortillas at a time and cook until golden, 2 to 3 minutes per side. Carefully remove the toothpicks or skewers and continue cooking on the other two sides until nicely browned. Sponge on absorbent paper. Cook the rest of the taquitos , adding more oil as needed.

In a serving platter , place the taquitos . Top with lettuce and serve with guacamole, salsa and sour cream, if desired.

Minced meat cutlets in theoven

Preparation time: 1 hr

Ingredients per 10 servings

Minced meat 500 gr

Potato2 piece.

Onion1 piece.

White bread70 gr

Milk 50 ml

Wheat flour50 gr

Salt to taste

Black ground pepperto taste

Vegetable oil1 table.l.

Garlic1 of tooth

Preparation

Let's make the ingredients. Do not be skeptical about the addition of minced potatoes, it will make the cutlets more juicy and tender, in addition, such patties will be even tastier and more satisfying, and if desired, they can be served without garnish. Meat twist on a meat grinder or use ready mince factory production, it is better to use minced pork and beef in equal parts. Cutlets exclusively from beef will turn dry, and pork-fat

Onions clean from husk and finely cut with a knife.

Potatoes are mine, cleaned and rubbed on a medium grater. Potato juice does not need to be pressed, the starch contained in potatoes will make the minced meat more plastic and sticky. A couple of pieces of white bread soaked in milk to swell it. warm it with a spoon into a homogeneous mass.

In a bowl with mince send chopped onion, passed through the press a clove of garlic and grated potatoes. Put the same bread and milk there. Add salt and black ground pepper to taste.

The mass is well mixed. It is believed that meat likes hands, so minced meat is better to stir with your hands. The minced meat for the meatballs should be juicy and slightly moist, if the milk gives insufficient moisture, you can add a little warm water. A couple of tablespoons are enough.

Form with wet hands patty. We roll them in flour or breadcrumbs.

Form for baking smeared with vegetable oil. Put on it the blanks of meatballs. The oven is heated to 180 degrees. Put in it the form with meatballs. First, you can cover it with foil, bake it for about 20 minutes, then remove the foil and bake for about 10 minutes. The cutlets should be well browned, but they should not be dried. Serve the cutlets with garnish or fresh vegetables. Enjoy your meal!

BBQ chicken skewers (thebest)

Preparation 20 min

Cooking 15 min

Maceration 24 hrs

Portions 4

Ingredients

Skewers

1/2 cup (125 ml) buttermilk

5 ml (1 tsp.) Onion powder

5 ml (1 teaspoon) of garlic powder

1/2 teaspoon (2.5 ml) ground allspice

1/2 teaspoon (2.5 ml) cayenne pepper

1 1/2 lb (675 g) boneless, skinless chicken breasts, cubed

6 green onions, sliced into 1 1/2 inch (4 cm) pieces (optional)

Barbecue sauce

60 ml (1/4 cup) ketchup

30 ml (2 tbsp.) Water

15 ml (1 tbsp.) Tomato paste

15 ml (1 tbsp.) Maple syrup

5 ml (1 teaspoon) sweet paprika

1/2 teaspoon (2.5 ml) ground coriander

1/4 teaspoon (1 ml) ground allspice

Vegetable oil, for brushing

Preparation

In a glass dish using a whisk, combine the buttermilk and the spices. Add the chicken. Salt and pepper. Cover and refrigerate 24 hours.

Barbecue sauce

Inside a glass bowl, add all ingredients with a whisk. Microwave 1 minute or until sauce is boiling. Reserve.

Preheat the barbecue to medium power. Oil the grid.

Drain the poultry and pat dry lightly. Discard the marinade. Thread cubes onto flat metal skewers, alternating with green onions, if desired. Lightly oil the skewers.

Grill the skewers for just 5 minutes per side. Brush the chicken with half the barbecue sauce and cook for 1 minute per side or until the meat is cooked through. Reserve on a plate and then cover with foil. Leave to rest for 5 minutes.

Serve the chicken kebabs with rice and a green salad, if desired. Serve with the remains of the barbecue sauce.

Grilled sesame chickendrumsticks and coleslaw

Preparation 15 min

Cooking 35 min

Portions 4

Ingredients

Chicken

1/4 cup (60 ml) hoisin sauce

45 ml (3 tbsp.) Ketchup

15 ml (1 tbsp.) Brown sugar

15 ml (1 tbsp.) Rice vinegar

10 ml (2 tsp.) Toasted sesame oil

10 ml (2 tsp.) Sambal oelek

1 kg (2.2 lb) chicken drumsticks with the skin on

Coleslaw

60 ml (1/4 cup) rice vinegar

30 ml (2 tbsp.) Fish sauce

15 ml (1 tbsp.) Brown sugar

10 ml (2 tsp.) Toasted sesame oil

340 g (4 cups) green cabbage, finely chopped on a mandolin

2 green onions, thinly sliced

30 ml (2 tbsp.) Black sesame seeds

Preparation

Preheat half the barbecue on high power and the other half on low power. Oil the grid.

In a bowl, whisk all ingredients except the chicken. Pepper. Add the chicken and toss to coat well with the marinade.

Place drumsticks on the soft section of the barbecue. Close the barbecue lid. Cook for 30 minutes, turning them several times during cooking. Reserve the marinade.

Meanwhile, in another bowl, combine all the ingredients. Let the cabbage macerate while the chicken cooks.

Brush the chicken with the marinade. Finish cooking on the raised section of the barbecue for 5 minutes or until the chicken is cooked through and golden brown.

NOTE

Serve with grilled corn chunks, if desired.

Marinated pork and pineapple tacos (tacos al pastor)

Preparation 40 min

Cooking 25 min

Maceration 4 hrs

Portions 4 to 6

Ingredients

4 dried guajillo peppers, seeded and cut into chunks (see note)

3 garlic cloves, halved

15 ml (1 tbsp.) Vegetable oil

5 ml (1 teaspoon) dried oregano

1/2 teaspoon (2.5 ml) ground allspice

1/2 teaspoon (2.5 ml) ground cumin

1/2 teaspoon (2.5 ml) ground black pepper

1/3 cup (75 ml) orange juice

60 ml (1/4 cup) red or white wine vinegar

1 1/2 lb (675 g) boneless pork shoulder without the rind, cut into 1/2-inch (1.5-cm) thick slices

1 large white onion, slice into 1/2-inch (1-cm) thick slices

1/2 pineapple without the peel, core removed and cut in half vertically

10 g (1/4 cup) chopped cilantro

12 soft corn tortillas, 10 cm (4 in.) In diameter, lightly toasted

Lime wedges, for serving

Preparation

Soften the garlic inside the oil in a saucepan over medium heat for 2 minutes. Cook for another 30 seconds after adding the spices. Combine the orange juice, vinegar, and rehydrated

peppers in a mixing bowl. Take to a boil, reduce to a low heat for 2 minutes. Allow to cool.

In a blender, reduce the mixture to a smooth puree. Pour into an airtight container.

In a glass dish or an airtight bag, place the meat and coat it with two-thirds of the marinade. Cover and let macerate for 4 to 6 hours in the refrigerator. Reserve the rest of the marinade in the refrigerator for serving.

Heat a ridged pan over high heat. Oil the pan. Grill the onion slices for 2 minutes per side. Reserve on a plate. Grill the pineapple quarters. Reserve on the plate with the onions. On a work surface, roughly chop the onion and mince the pineapple. Reserve in separate bowls.

Grill half the meat at a time on one side, 6 to 8 minutes or until very crisp. Salt. Turn it over and cook for like 1 minute.

On a work surface, layer a few slices of grilled meat at a time and thinly slice them. Place in a warm plate until ready to serve.

Place the onion, pineapple, cilantro, reserved marinade, tortillas, grilled pork and lime wedges in the center of the table. Let each person top their tacos.

NOTE

Guajillo chili peppers are a variety of dried chili peppers commonly used in Mexican cuisine. It can be found in specialty grocery stores. Alternatively, you can replace the 4 guajillo peppers in the recipe with 1 peeled roasted pepper and 1 fresh chili and omit step 1.

Grilled tomatillo salsa

PREPARATION 15 MIN

COOKING 20 MIN

Yield 500 ml (2 cups)

Ingredients

1 1/2 lb (675 g) fresh tomatillos, unpeeled

1 small onion, thinly sliced

1 jalapeño pepper, seeded and halved

1 garlic clove, cut in half

15 ml (1 tbsp.) Vegetable oil

70 g (2 cups) cilantro leaves and stems, chopped

Preparation

Put the grill at the center of the oven. Preheat oven to 180 ° C (350 ° F).

Remove the outer shell covering the tomatillos. Wash them well under lukewarm water to get rid of the sticky substance on the membrane. Cut the tomatillos into quarters.

On a non-stick or foil-lined baking sheet, toss the tomatillos, onion, chili and garlic with oil. Salt and pepper. Bake for 10 minutes. Stir the vegetables. Increasing the power of the grill oven (broil). Continue cooking for 15 minutes, until the onions are tender and the tomatillos begin to blacken. Let cool.

In a food processor, chop the cilantro with the vegetables for a few seconds to maintain a coarse salsa texture. Using a spatula, scrape the sides a few times. Adjust seasoning.

Serve warm or cold. Goes very well with nachos, tacos or white fish. Salsa will keep for 1 week in an airtight container in the refrigerator.

Meat in soy sauce in the oven

Preparation time:

2 hours 30 mins

Ingredients For 4 Servings

Pork loin 500 gr

MARINADE:garlic3 of tooth.

Soy 2

vegetable oil1

honey 1

basil 1

Thyme, thyme 0.5 gr.ch.

Lemon zest0.5 gr.ch.

Dry spices 0.2

Preparation

How to marinate meat in soy sauce? Prepare the products for the marinade. I have a certain set, but you can change it by adding or removing some ingredients. What you're going to make marinade doesn't really matter, so you can use your own, tested and loved one.

Peel the garlic and chop it finely with a knife. You can apply the garlic press or instead of slicing crush the cloves with the side of the knife. Also for this purpose will be suitable mortar and pestle.

Rub the lemon zest on a small grater. In a bowl, mix soy sauce, honey, vegetable oil, crushed garlic. Add the lemon zest and dried herbs to the marinade. Mix everything thoroughly.

Wash the pork, dry and cut into pieces about 1 cm thick.

Beat each slice of pork well with a hammer on both sides. If the meat has a white film on the sides, cut it in several places with a knife - it will prevent the meat from bending "cup" in the process of baking.

Fold the chops into a bowl of suitable size. And pour the pork marinade, trying to distribute it all over the meat surface. It is good if the pork will be immersed in marinade at least partially.

The meat in a bowl with marinade tighten with food film and remove for 1-2 hours in the refrigerator. When the time is out, cover the baking dish with parchment.

Put the beaten meat on parchment. Top with the marinade. It will keep the dish from drying out when baking. Try to water meat, not paper. Place the pork in a preheated oven to 180 degrees Celsius and bake for about 35 minutes. Then turn on the top grill and brown it for about 10 minutes. Determine the exact time and temperature of baking by your oven!

Serve the finished meat in the soy sauce immediately, while it is hot, with any garnish. Enjoy your meal!

To the meat during baking does not dry out on top (from

below it is surrounded by juice and marinade released from it), it is necessary to periodically grease its sauce from the bottom of the form.

Keep in mind that the ovens are different for everyone. The temperature and cooking time may differ from those mentioned in the recipe. To make any baked dish successful, use useful information about the features of the oven!

The best choice for this recipe is fresh pork tenderloin or fillet. The meat should be tender and without "fibers", then the finished chop will literally melt in the mouth. It is better to refuse meat on the bone at once.
I usually take portion pork chops, or a piece of carbonade without bone and cut it with slices of the desired thickness.

Pork rolls stuffed in the oven

Ingredients for 4 servings

change the line-upunits

Pork loin 1 kg

Canned mushrooms 170 gr

Onion 1 piece.

Garlic1 of tooth.

Flour1

Sour cream3

Hard cheese 50 gr

Vegetable oil2

Saltto taste

Black ground pepperto taste

Preparation time:

1 hour 45 mins

Preparation

How to make pork rolls with mushroom filling? Prepare all the necessary products. For rolls I took four pieces of loin about 2-3 cm wide, you can use the neck of pork. Mushrooms will be suitable canned, or you can take fresh mushrooms.

If you have a loin on the bone, cut the bones, and the pulp is well beat with a hammer. For the convenience of beating, place a piece of meat in a plastic bag, so there will be no extra spray and your kitchen will remain as clean as possible. The thinner you get a piece of meat, the more convenient it will be to make rolls out of it.

Peel the garlic and rub it on a shallow grate, or pass through the garlic. Add half a serving of sour cream to the garlic, a pinch of salt and mix well.

The resulting mixture smear with a thin layer of each piece of meat. Leave for a while, 10-15 minutes will be enough.

Meanwhile, prepare the filling. Cut the canned mushrooms into small fragments. Peel the onion and chop them in small cubes.

In a thick-bottomed frying pan, heat the vegetable oil. Send the mushrooms and onions to fry. Cook over high heat until golden. Do not forget to stir periodically, otherwise the filling will burn. I cooked for about five minutes.

Add the flour to the pan and stir immediately to prevent lumps. In a minute send 1-1.5 tbsp. sour cream to the filling and salt to taste. Stir, after a few seconds remove the pan from the stove.

Spread the chop meat on the surface of the kitchen table, sprinkle evenly with ground black or fragrant pepper, spread the mushroom filling on top with an even layer. I got 1 tablespoon with a slide for each piece.

Roll the pork into a roll. Do the same with the remaining chops and stuffing.

Put the ready-made pork rolls in a baking dish. The bottom of the mold I do not grease with vegetable oil, in the process of baking it formed a sufficient amount of filling and sour cream, so the rolls do not burn.

Put the mold in the oven, set the top-bottom mode and bake at 180-220 degrees for about an hour (depending on the capabilities of your oven). Then sprinkle the rolls with grated cheese and send to bake again for 7-10 minutes.

Garnish with fresh finely chopped greens.

To make the rolls as juicy as possible, cover the form with foil before baking. Cook in this way for 30-40 minutes, then remove the foil and bake until cooked and browned. I usually don't use foil to make rolls.

If desired, you can exclude step number 3 and 4, and pieces of chops only slightly salt and

pepper. Then the finished rolls will be a little less oily and without the aroma of garlic.

Enjoy your

appetite!

Grilled vegetable sandwich

Ingredients

baguette with bran

1/2Eggplant

1/2Zucchini

1tomato

50 mlvegetable oil

pinch of dry spices for vegetables

2-3 tbsp.pesto sauce

handful of arugula

salt, pepper

Preparation

Wash the vegetables and cut into 0.5 cm thick circles.

Mix butter, spices for vegetables, salt, pepper. Dip the eggplant and zucchini into the spicy butter.

Heat a grill pan well and fry the vegetables on both sides. Then place on a paper towel to remove excess oil.

Cut 2 pieces from the baguette 12-14 cm long. On the bottom halves put pesto sauce, grilled vegetables, tomato circles, arugula.

Cover with the top halves of the baguette and serve.

Grilled corn on the barbecue (Elotes a la parrilla)

Preparation 25 min

Cooking 12 min

Yield 6

Ingredients

60 ml (¼ cup) sour cream

60 ml (¼ cup) mayonnaise

15 ml (1 tbsp.) Chopped fresh cilantro

1 garlic clove, finely chopped

5 ml (1 tsp.) Chili seasoning

6 ears of fresh corn with leaves

60 g (½ cup) crumbled queso fresco or feta cheese (see note above)

1 lime, cut into wedges

Salt and pepper

Preparation

In a bowl, add sour cream, mayonnaise, cilantro, garlic and chili seasoning. Salt and pepper. Refrigerate until ready to serve.

Peel the ears of corn without completely detaching the leaves, that is to say by folding them towards the stalk in order to release all the corn. Remove all silks. Tie the leaves with butcher's twine. The leaves will serve as a support when serving the corn.

Preheat half of the barbecue on high power. Oil the grid.

Place the cobs on the lit section of the barbecue so that the leaves are not in direct contact with the fire. Close the barbecue lid. Grill the corn for about 12 minutes, turning them a few times or until tender and golden. Place on a serving platter.

When ready to serve, brush the cobs with the sour cream mixture. Sprinkle with cheese and then drizzle with lime juice.

NOTE

Take a look at the video Preparing a corn on the cob for grilling.

Out of season, if you don't have access to fresh leaf corn, you can insert a stick into the cob to create a support. Disposable wooden sushi sticks are a good option.

Grilled Vegetable Salsa

Preparation 25 min

Cooking 10 minutes

Yield 750 ml (3 cups)

Ingredients

8 italian tomatoes, halved

6 green onions, cut into 2-inch (5-cm) pieces

1 jalapeño pepper, halved and seeded

15 ml (1 tbsp.) Olive oil

15 g (1/2 cup) fresh cilantro, chopped

30 ml (2 tbsp.) Lime juice

1 ml (1/4 teaspoon) ground cumin

Salt and pepper

Preparation

Place the rack inside the upper third of the oven. Preheat grill oven (broil). Line a baking sheet with foil.

On the baking sheet, then place tomatoes, green onions and chili peppers. Oil, salt and pepper. Place tomatoes and chili, cut side down on baking sheet.

Bake for like 10 minutes or until the vegetables are charred. Let cool.

In a food processor, finely chop the green onions and chili pepper. Add the tomatoes and mix just enough so that they are chopped. Transfer to a bowl. Add the cilantro, lime juice and cumin. Adjust seasoning.

Serve warm or cold with corn chips. Salsa will keep for like 1 week in the refrigerator.

Avocado and grilled corn salsa

Preparation 15 min

Cooking 10 minutes

Yield 625 ml (2 1/2 cups), approximately

Ingredients

2 ears of corn, peeled

1 firm but ripe avocado, peeled and diced

30 ml (2 tbsp.) Lime juice

10 g (¼ cup) coarsely chopped cilantro

1 green onion, finely chopped

½ jalapeño pepper, seeded and finely chopped

Preparation

Preheat the barbecue on high power. Oil the grid.

In a pot of salted clean boiling water, cook the ears for about 2 minutes. Remove, drain and pat dry.

Grill the ears for 3 to 4 minutes or until golden, rolling them with tongs. Let cool on a board. Using a knife, shell the corn. In a bowl, add avocado including lime juice. Add the corn kernels and the rest of the ingredients. Salt and pepper. Serve with corn chips.

NOTE

This salsa would be delicious with grilled white fish or as a garnish in fajitas. It would also go very well with fish and chips.

Grilled pork tacos

Preparation 25 min

Cooking 12 min

Maceration 12 pm

Portions 4

Ingredients

1/2 cup (125 ml) chili sauce

45 ml (3 tbsp.) Molasses

30 ml (2 tbsp.) Of tabasco with chipotle pepper

30 ml (2 tbsp.) Of chili powder

1 1/2 lb (675 g) of pork flank steak or pork tenderloin

12 taco shells

The flesh of 1 avocado, diced

2 small tomatoes, diced

1 cup (250 ml) grated sharp cheddar cheese

1 yellow bell pepper, well seeded and thinly sliced

Sour cream to taste

Salt and pepper

Preparation

In a bowl, mix all the ingredients.

In another bowl, coat the flank steak well with 1/3 cup (75 ml) of the sauce. Cover and refrigerate at least 1 night. Refrigerate the rest of the sauce.

Preheat the barbecue to medium power. Oil the grid.

Grill the meat for like 5 minutes per side or until pink. For the pork tenderloins, the cooking will take a little longer. Salt and pepper. Brush with the marinade a few times during cooking. Reserve on a plate. Cover with foil and let stand for about 10 minutes. Thinly slice.

In a small saucepan or make use of a microwave, heat the remaining sauce.

Place the meat, sauce and the rest of the ingredients in separate bowls in the center of the table and let guests garnish the shells themselves.

BBQ Bacon Dill SpaghettiSquash Quiches

Preparation 20 min

Cooking 1 hour

Portions 4

Ingredients

1 2.2 lb (1 kg) spaghetti squash (see note)

15 ml (1 tbsp.) Olive oil

6 eggs

1/2 cup (125 ml) 15% cream

30 ml (2 tbsp.) Chopped dill

3 slices of bacon, sliced into 1/2-inch (1-cm) strips

Preparation

Preheat half of the barbecue on high power.

Cut the squash in half lengthwise. Using a spoon, remove seeds including filaments. Brush the inside with the oil. Salt and pepper. Wrap each squash half tightly in foil.

Place the squash halves cut side down on the lit side of the barbecue. Close the lid and cook for 15 minutes or until the squash begins to soften by turning it halfway through cooking.

Meanwhile, inside a bowl, whisk eggs with the cream and dill. Salt and pepper.

On a work surface, open the foil on the cut surface of the squash while keeping the rest of the foil that covers the skin of the squash. Using a fork, scrape the flesh to fray without puncturing the skin. Place the squash halves on a plate. Pour the egg mixture inside. Divide the bacon strips on top.

Carefully place the squash halves on the unlit side of the barbecue. Close the barbecue lid. Bake for like 45 minutes or until the egg mixture puffs and is firm to the center, maintaining a temperature of 200 ° C (400 ° F). Let stand 5 minutes on a plate. Cut the squash halves in half. Serve with a green salad, if desired.

NOTE

Choose a squash without cracks to avoid any leakage of the egg mixture.

Grilled Tofu Beet Salad, Greek Yogurt Dressing

Preparation 30 min

Cooking 6 min

Maceration 2 hours

Portions 4

Ingredients

30 ml (2 tbsp.) Olive oil

15 ml (1 tbsp.) Honey

15 ml (1 tbsp.) Lemon juice

1 garlic clove, finely chopped

1/4 teaspoon (1 ml) crushed pepper flakes

1 lb (450 g) extra-firm tofu, cut into 1/2-inch (1 cm) thick slices crosswise

1/2 cup (125 ml) plain 2% greek yogurt (see notes)

4 cooked beets (see notes), thinly sliced on a mandolin

1/2 small red onion, minced

15 ml (1 tbsp.) Olive oil

5 ml (1 teaspoon) lemon juice

1/2 english cucumber, thinly sliced on a mandolin

30 ml (2 tbsp.) Chopped dill

1/2 teaspoon (2.5 ml) ground sumac

Preparation

In a 28 x 20 cm (that's 11 x 8-inch) glass dish, combine the oil, honey, lemon juice, garlic and chili. Salt and pepper. Add the tofu and coat it well with the marinade. Cover and let macerate for 2 hours in the refrigerator.

Preheat the barbecue on high power. Oil the grid.

Remove the tofu slices from marinade and set them aside on a plate. Whisk the Greek yogurt into the marinade. Adjust seasoning. Scoop 45 ml (3 tbsp.) Of the dressing for the salad. Grill the tofu slices for 2 minutes on one side. Turn them over, then brush with the remaining Greek yogurt sauce. Continue cooking for 2 minutes. Reserve on the plate.

In a bowl, combine the beets, onion, oil and lemon juice. Salt and pepper. Divide on a serving platter. Rinse the bowl. Combine cucumber, dill and reserved Greek yogurt sauce. Spread over the beets. Add the tofu and sprinkle with sumac.

NOTE

We opted for an Oikos® 2% Greek yogurt, which gives the tofu a slightly creamy side in addition to a liquid enough texture for the dressing.

You can cook your beets yourself for 1 hour in a saucepan of water and peel them or opt for a shortcut by using a 500 g bag of already cooked beets that you find in grocery stores.

Grilled flank steak, orangeyogurt and curry marinade

Preparation 25 min

Cooking 20 min

Maceration 8 h

Portions 4

Ingredients

1/2 cup (125 ml) 11% yogurt (see note)

1/3 cup (75 ml) orange juice

30 ml (2 tbsp.) Honey

30 ml (2 tbsp.) Harissa

10 ml (2 tsp.) Curry powder

1/2 teaspoon (2.5 ml) garlic powder

1/2 teaspoon (2.5 ml) ground ginger

1 1/2 lb (675 g) of flank steak, cut into 4 steaks

2 small red onions, slice into 1/2-inch (1 cm) thick rings

30 ml (2 tbsp.) Olive oil

5 ml (1 teaspoon) red or white wine vinegar

4 small zucchini, halved lengthwise

4 naan breads

10 g (1/4 cup) chopped cilantro

Preparation

In a large bowl, put all your ingredients with a whisk, except for the flank steak. Salt and pepper. Take half of the sauce in a small bowl. Cover and refrigerate until ready to serve.

Add the flank steak to the large bowl of marinade and coat well. Cover and let macerate for 8 hours in the refrigerator.

Preheat the barbecue on high power. Oil the grid.

Place the onions in the center of a large sheet of aluminum foil. Drizzle with half the oil and vinegar. Salt and pepper.

Close tightly in foil. Oil the zucchini with the rest of the oil. Salt and pepper.

Drain the meat and set aside on a plate. Discard the marinade. Place the papillote on barbecue grill and then cook for 15 minutes, turning it halfway through cooking. At the same time, grill the steaks 5 minutes per side for rare doneness or to desired doneness. Set aside on a plate and then let stand for 5 minutes. Grill the zucchini for like 3 minutes on each side. Grill the naan breads for like 1 minute on each side.

On a work surface, slice the meat. Serve the flank steak with the zucchini, onions and naan breads. Garnish with cilantro and serve with the reserved yogurt sauce.

Grilled chicken, Greek yogurtand smoked paprika marinade

Preparation 15 min

Cooking 40 min

Maceration 8 h

Portions 4

Ingredients

3/4 cup (180 ml) 0% greek yogurt (see note)

30 ml (2 tbsp.) Olive oil

15 ml (1 tbsp.) Red wine vinegar

15 ml (1 tbsp.) Tomato paste

10 ml (2 tsp.) Smoked paprika

5 ml (1 teaspoon) of garlic powder

5 ml (1 teaspoon) of salt

1/2 teaspoon (2.5 ml) ground pepper

0.5 ml (1/8 teaspoon) cayenne pepper

4 chicken thighs, bone and skin on

4 chicken drumsticks with the skin on

Preparation

In a bowl, whisk all the ingredients except the chicken. Add the chicken and coat well with the marinade. Cover and let macerate in the refrigerator for 8 hours.

Preheat half of the barbecue on high power. Oil the grid.

Drain the chicken and discard the marinade. Oil the meat. Place the chicken on the unlit section of the barbecue, skin side down on the grill. Close the barbecue lid. Cook for 20 minutes.

Flip the chicken and continue cooking for 15 minutes or until the chicken is cooked through. Finish cooking by quickly grilling the chicken skin side down over the lit section. Serve with a green salad, if desired.

Note

Oikos® 0% fat greek yogurt is perfect for marinating chicken, but you can also use 2% or 11% greek yogurt, depending on what you have on hand.

Pizza on naan bread with marinated vegetables and barbecued eggs

Preparation 20 min

Cooking 15 min

Portions 4

Ingredients

4 eggs

4 naan breads

125 ml (1/2 cup) sweet store-bought pepper spread

1 250 ml jar of various grilled vegetables in oil, drained and coarsely chopped

1 250 ml jar of marinated mini artichokes, drained and halved

2 balls of 100 g each of mozzarella di bufala cheese , torn into small pieces

45 ml (3 tbsp.) Pesto

Finely grated fresh parmesan cheese, to taste

Preparation

Preheat the barbecue on high power to obtain a heat of 315 ° C (600 ° F).

Individually wrap the eggs in absorbent paper soaked in water, then wrap them tightly with aluminum foil.

Place the eggs on the wire rack. Close the barbecue and cook for 14 minutes for a well-cooked yolk. Remove the eggs. Close the barbecue and set it to medium power, around 200 ° C (400 ° F). Remove the foil then rinse the eggs under cold water for 1 minute. Remove the shell without breaking the egg. Reserve.

Spread the spread on the breads. Distribute the vegetables, mozzarella and pesto.

Cover the grill with foil (see note). Bake pizzas directly on foil for 5 minutes or until cheese is slightly melted and bottoms of buns are crisp.

Cut the eggs into quarters and place them on the pizzas. Sprinkle with Parmesan.

NOTE

Cover the barbecue grill with aluminum foil to prevent the breads from being too dark and to make it easier to remove the pizzas after they are cooked.

The new RICARDO "the Rock" plate can also be used on the barbecue.

Beef keftas, tabbouleh andsumac sauce

Preparation 35 min

Cooking 10 minutes

Waiting 15 min

Portions 4

Ingredients

1/2 cup (125 ml) mayonnaise

1/2 cup (125 ml) Greek yogurt

5 mL (1 tsp.) Ground sumac

250 ml (1 cup) water

1/4 teaspoon (1 ml) salt

180 g (1 cup) fine bulgur

70 g (1 1/2 cups) chopped parsley

5 green onions, chopped

280 g (2 cups) cherry tomatoes, halved

60 ml (1/4 cup) olive oil

1 lemon, for juice

10 mint leaves, chopped

1 garlic clove, chopped

450 g (1 lb) lean ground beef

2 garlic cloves, chopped

1 lemon, grated zest only

1/2 teaspoon (2.5 ml) salt

1/2 teaspoon (2.5 ml) ground coriander

1/2 teaspoon (2.5 ml) ground cumin

1/2 teaspoon (2.5 ml) ground allspice

Cayenne or Aleppo pepper, to taste

Preparation

In a small bowl, put all the ingredients. Salt and pepper. Reserve.

In a saucepan, bring the water and salt to a boil. Remove from fire. Add the bulgur. Cover and let swell for 15 minutes. Break up the grains with a fork and transfer to a bowl. Add the parsley and green onions. Transfer half of the bulgur mixture to another bowl.

In one of the bulgur bowls, add the cherry tomatoes, oil, lemon juice, mint and garlic. Add salt, pepper and mix well. Reserve.

In the second bowl of the bulgur mixture, add the beef, garlic, lemon zest, salt and spices. Mix well. Divide the mixture into 8 parts. With lightly oiled hands, form one piece of meat at a time into a 5-inch (12.5 cm) long sausage around skewers or sushi chopsticks or shape them without support. Reserve on a large plate. Lightly oil the meat.

Preheat the barbecue on high power. Oil the grid.Cook 8 to 10 minutes, turning frequently or until meat is cooked through. Serve the keftas with tabbouleh, sumac sauceand pita breads, if desired.

Grilled cauliflower with curry, coconut and pomegranate condiment

Preparation 20 Min

Cooking 20 Min

Portions 4 To 6

Ingredients

Coconut condiment

1/4 cup (20 g) grated unsweetened coconut

5 ml (1 teaspoon) of butter

10 ml (2 teaspoons) of honey

1/2 teaspoon (2.5 ml) curry powder

125 ml (cup) 10% plain yogurt

1/4 cup (60 ml) coconut cream (see note)

15 ml (1 tbsp.) Chopped dill

1/4 cup (55 g) butter, melted

10 ml (2 tsp.) Curry powder

1 cauliflower, cut into large florets

1 Lebanese cucumber, sliced in half lengthwise then sliced

45 g (1/4 cup) pomegranate seeds

15 ml (1 tbsp.) Lime juice

15 ml (1 tbsp.) Chopped dill

Preparation

In a small skillet with medium heat, brown the coconut in the butter with the honey and curry. Reserve.

In a bowl, combine the yogurt including the coconut cream and dill.

Preheat the barbecue on high power.

In another bowl, put the butter and curry. Add the cauliflower and coat well. Salt and pepper. Layer 2 sheets of aluminum foil. In the center, place the cauliflower. Close the foil tightly. Place the papillote on the barbecue grill. Close the lid and then cook for 10 minutes or until the cauliflower is al dente. Open the foil and transfer the cauliflower to the wire rack. Cook the cauliflower florets until they are well caramelized or almost blackened, about 2 minutes per side (see note). Keep warm.

In another bowl, put the cucumber, pomegranate seeds and lime juice. Salt and pepper.

In a serving dish, spread the yogurt mixture. Top with the cauliflower and the garnish with the cucumber mixture. Sprinkle with dill and garnish with coconut condiment.

Delicious with lamb or pork chops.

NOTE

You want the solid part of a 398 ml (14 oz) can of coconut milk (do not use light coconut milk). It is best to refrigerate the can

8 hours before, the fat will be stronger and easier to separate. Use the milk for another purpose, such as in a smoothie or soup.

We want the cauliflower to be almost burnt. Well blackened without being charred.

Barbecue spilled apricots

Preparation 20 min

Cooking 25 min

Yield 12 servings

Ingredients

150 g (1 cup) unbleached all-purpose flour

1/2 teaspoon of (2.5 ml) baking soda

1/4 teaspoon (1 ml) salt

1/4 cup (55 g) of unsalted butter, softened

105 g (1/2 cup) sugar

1 tempered egg

1/2 cup (125 ml) milk

80 g (6 tbsp.) Sugar

6 ripe firm apricots, halved with pitted or 1 can (398 ml (14 oz.) Of apricots, halved in light syrup, drained (see note)

Preparation

Preheat the barbecue on high power. Generously butter the 12 cavities of a non-stick muffin pan.

In a bowl, combine the flour, baking soda and salt.

In another bowl, cream the butter and sugar with an electric mixer until the mixture whitens. Add the egg, whisking until the mixture is smooth. Incorporate the dry ingredients alternately with the milk. Reserve.

Pour 7.5 ml (1 teaspoon) of sugar in each cavity of the muffin tin. Place the apricot halves cut side down, then spread the dough.

Turn off a section of the barbecue. Place pan on the unlit section of the barbecue. Close the lid and bake 25 minutes or until a toothpick inserted in the center of a cake comes out clean, maintaining a heat of 200 ° C (400 ° F) and turning the pan on top. even halfway through cooking.

Pass a thin blade between the wall of each cavity and cakes. Invert the mold onto a baking sheet to unmold the cakes. Replace the apricot halves if necessary. Delicious hot with ice cream or coconut yogurt.

NOTE

Fresh apricots sometimes cook too quickly and mash. Choose them ripe, but still firm. Canned apricots are very useful for this dessert.

Barbecued chocolate pudding

Preparation 20 min

Cooking 50 min

Yield 6 servings

Ingredients

Chocolate sauce

140 g (2/3 cup) brown sugar

20 g (3 tbsp.) Cocoa powder, sifted

5 ml (1 teaspoon) of cornstarch

310 ml (1 1/4 cups) water

1/4 cup (60 ml) 35% cream

1/2 teaspoon of (2.5 ml) vanilla extract

115 g (3/4 cup) unbleached all-purpose flour

1/4 cup (25 g) cocoa, sifted

1/4 teaspoon (1 ml) baking soda

1 pinch of salt

1/4 cup (55 g) unsalted butter, melted

140 g (2/3 cup) sugar

1 egg

3/4 cup (180 ml) milk

2 oz (55 g) 70% dark chocolate, roughly chopped

Preparation

Chocolate sauce

In a 25 cm (10 inch) diameter cast iron skillet with a capacity of 2 liters (8 cups), whisk together the brown sugar, cocoa and cornstarch. Add the water, cream and vanilla while stirring. On the stove over medium heat, bring to a boil until well combined. Let cool.

Preheat half of the barbecue to medium power.

Cake

In a bowl, put the flour, cocoa, baking soda and salt.

In another bowl, whisk the butter, sugar and egg until well combined. Using a spatula, incorporate the dry ingredients alternately with the milk. Add the chocolate.

Using a large ice cream scoop, spread the batter over the warm chocolate sauce.

Place the pan on the unlit section of the barbecue. Close lid and bake 40 minutes or until a toothpick inserted in the center of the cake comes out clean, maintaining a heat of 190 ° C (375 ° F). Let stand 15 minutes before serving.

Barbecued peaches and raspberries

Preparation 15 min

Cooking 5 min

Portions 4

Ingredients

405 g (3 cups) fresh raspberries (see note)

40 g (3 tbsp.) Sugar

6 small ripe peaches, halved and pitted (see note)

4 scoops of vanilla ice cream

Preparation

In a blender, puree 270 g (2 cups) of the raspberries and sugar to a smooth purée. Over a bowl, pass the mash through a sieve. Compost the seeds. Reserve the coulis.

Preheat the barbecue on high power. Oil the grid.

Grill the peaches for 3 mins per side or until heated through. In soup plates, distribute the raspberry coulis. Place 3 peach halves then a scoop of ice cream. Distribute the rest of the raspberries.

NOTE

For the coulis, you can replace the fresh raspberries with frozen and thawed raspberries.

You can also replace the fresh peaches with 1 can of 28 oz (796 ml) halved peaches in light syrup, drained. As they are larger, put only 2 halves per person. The cooking time remains the same.

Shrimp and piperade skewers

Preparation 15 min

Cooking 25 min

Portions 4

Ingredients

1 onion, thinly sliced

2 garlic cloves, chopped

60 ml (1/4 cup) olive oil

4 peppers of various colors, seeded and thinly sliced

2 tomatoes, diced

Shrimp skewers

1 1/2 lb (675 g) large shrimp (8-12) with shell

30 ml (2 tbsp.) Olive oil

15 ml (1 tbsp.) Sweet paprika

15 ml (1 tbsp.) White wine vinegar

Preparation

Soften the onion, garlic into the oil in a large pot over medium heat. Cook for another 5 minutes after adding the peppers. Cook for 15 minutes, or until the peppers are soft, before adding the tomatoes. Season with salt and pepper.

Meanwhile, whisk together all of the ingredients in a large

mixing bowl. Season with salt and pepper. Using skewers, thread the shrimp onto the skewers.

Preheat the barbecue on high power. Oil the grid.

Grill the shrimp skewers 2 minutes per side or until cooked through.

Serve the piperade with the skewers. Also delicious with sliced roasted potatoes or toasted country bread.

NOTE

Why keep the shell if we take it off the plate? Because barbecued shrimp will be much softer, juicier, and won't stick to the grill.

Of Basque origin, the piperade is a dish composed of peppers, onions, tomatoes and chili peppers.

Marinade for pork andchicken

5 min

Ingredients

3 tbsp Massalé (or massala), in good grocery stores)

6 tbsp Vegetable oil (no olive oil)

4 tbsp Honey

2 pods Garlic

1 Onion

4 tbsp Soya sauce

Preparation

Total time: 5 min

Preparation: 5 min

STEP 1

Peel the onion and garlic.

STEP 2

Place in the food processor bowl.

STEP 3

Mixer.

STEP 4

Add the honey, soy sauce, oil and garam massed one after the other, still mixing.

STEP 5

It's ready. Soak pork ribs, chicken thighs, or small pieces of pork or chicken for skewers, for at least 3/4 h (more is better).

STEP 6

Cook the meat on barbecue, basting it with the marinade left at the bottom of the dish (or not, it depends on your shape in front of the barbecue!)

Meat in salt in the oven

Ingredients for 8 servings

Pork 900 gr

Salt 1 kg

Bollocks 1 thyme,

Thyme 1 gr.ch.

Rosemary dry 1 gr.ch.

Oregano dry 1 gr.ch.

Pepper peas 10

Preparation time: 1 hour 10 mins

Preparation

In such a convenient and original way, you can bake not only meat, but also fish, as well as chicken. In our family of all kinds of meat more respected pork. So we'll bake the pork carbonate. Soft parts of the carcass are suitable for baking in the oven, so the ham, spatula or loin will also be perfect. It is important that in the selected piece of meat there is no film, veins, no excessive fat. The main thing is that the meat was fresh or chilled.

Let's take a kilo of salt. For meat dishes it is better to choose salt of medium or large grinding, as well as sea salt with a mixture of peppers. Pour salt into a container in which it will be conveniently mixed. Add all the dry spices and pepper peas. Spices can be taken any. Perfectly combined with pork rosemary and black pepper peas. To them I added morethyme and oregano. Stir.

Beat one raw egg and mix well. You can do without an egg, but thanks to the egg salt shell will be better to keep the shape.

Take a baking dish, put on the bottom one third of the fragrant salt. It's going to be a substrate for our meat.

Meat should not be pre-prepared. Just take a piece of good fillet and put it on the salt substrate.

From above, fill the meat with the remaining salt, forming a slide. We're a little bit with our hands.

Put the meat to bake in a preheated to 180-200 degrees oven for one hour. After the time immediately do not get the meat from the salt shell, and give the meat in it to cool a little. Then break the shell with a knife. The salt hardens, the shell is very easily split and removed.

I've already cooked fish this way, and now I've decided to try meat. So, it's not checked once! Meat in salt - it is very tasty and simple! And most importantly, a dish cooked in this way is simply not possible to oversalt!

You can serve such meat as an independent dish, and with a side

dish. Very tasty sandwiches are made of it. A useful

replacement of sausage.

Have a nice

meal!

Conclusion

How much effort you have to do when cleaning depends heavily on your grill. Gas and electric grills are a lot easier to look after than charcoal grills because, in most cases, the former have collecting trays for the dripping fat. These are easier to clean and often even fit in the dishwasher.

Special grill cleaners are available to keep the body of your grill in good condition. It is better not to dye the surface - many grills are made of porcelain enamel, which does not adhere well to varnish or wax when it is hot.

The grill grate gets the most off when roasting: meat residues, fat and spices get stuck and form a black crust. You should therefore treat it to a special cleaning after every barbecue party and barbecue evening. As a soaking aid, you can use newspaper, which you wrap around the grate when it is damp and leave to work for a few hours. When the crust has loosened a little, you can remove the last residue with asponge and washing-up liquid. You can likewise achieve the same effect with natural help: simply place the grate on the nearby meadow overnight. The moisture and dew dissolve stubborn dirt overnight. A stainless steel grille can also withstand a wash cycle in the dishwasher.

An onion should also ensure a sparkling clean grate: Simply

rub one half of the onion over the grate while it is still hot. If you rub vigorously, you will remove any incrustations with ease. Great side effect: The onion disinfects and, according to the cleaning portal Helpling.de, is even supposed to remove invisible dirt.

When grilling with charcoal, it is also a good idea to use the remaining ash as a cleaning agent. You dip a damp cloth into the powdered remains and use it to sand off the crust. However, you can save a lot of work if you rub the grate with oil or fat before grilling.

With a little luck, even particularly old and encrusted grill grids can be cleaned again with the help of an oven cleaner. When you have rubbed the grate onto the grate, simply place it in a plastic bag for a few hours to soak in.

By the way: Coffee grounds are a natural alternative to give your old grille a shine again. Coffee works like sandpaper - just put it on a sponge after Sunday breakfast and rub the grill grate with it.

The ash pan also needs to be cleaned properly: Let the ash cool down well and then throw it in the general rubbish. The pot is swept with a hand brush and wiped with a damp cloth. Don't forget: dry the pot afterwards; otherwise, rust could form due to the moisture.

You can protect the lid from grease streaks with a soapy steel wool cushion after wiping over again with vinegar water and rinse clear.

Hibernating the grill: How to make your grill winterproof
After the barbecue season is before the barbecue season. Don't just put your grill in the basement after the summer - the moisture in the ash could cause the expensive piece to rust. Remove the ash and clean the grill thoroughly: soak the removable parts in a mixture of water and washing up liquid for two to three hours, then scrub with a sponge.

The clean grill must now be stored in a dry place, for example, in the cellar. To do this, put a cardboard box or bag over the grill. This protects it from dust, and it is ready for use again with the first warm ray

Lightning Source UK Ltd.
Milton Keynes UK
UKHW020634220621
385949UK00001B/61

9 786156 305657